ABSOLUTE BEGINNERS
Ukulele
BOOK TWO

WISE PUBLICATIONS
part of The Music Sales Group
London/New York/Paris/Sydney/Copenhagen/Berlin/Madrid/Tokyo

Published by
Wise Publications
14-15 Berners Street,
London W1T 3LJ, UK.

Exclusive Distributors:
Music Sales Limited
Distribution Centre,
Newmarket Road,
Bury St Edmunds,
Suffolk IP33 3YB, UK.
Music Sales Corporation
257 Park Avenue South,
New York,
NY 10010, USA.
Music Sales Pty Limited
20 Resolution Drive,
Caringbah, NSW 2229,
Australia.

Order No. AM996072
ISBN 978-1-84772-850-0
This book © Copyright 2009
Wise Publications, a division of Music Sales Limited.

Written by Steven Sproat
Edited by Fiona Bolton
Cover and book design by Chloë Alexander
Photography by Matthew Ward
Printed in the EU

CD recorded, mixed and mastered by Jonas Persson
Ukulele by Steven Sproat
Backing tracks by Paul Honey

Your Guarantee of Quality:
As publishers, we strive to produce every book to the highest
commercial standards.

The music has been freshly engraved and the book has been
carefully designed to minimise awkward page turns and to make
playing from it a real pleasure.

Throughout, the printing and binding have been planned
to ensure a sturdy, attractive publication which should give years
of enjoyment.

If your copy fails to meet our high standards, please inform us
and we will gladly replace it.

www.musicsales.com

Contents

Introduction

Welcome to *Absolute Beginners Ukulele Book Two*.
In **Book One** we covered the basics of playing the
ukulele. You learnt

- The correct position in which to sit or stand to
  play the ukulele
- The names of the strings
- How to hold down a chord
- A basic strumming technique including
  downstrokes and upstrokes
- How to count beats and play simple songs
- A fingerpicking pattern for songs with three
  beats to a bar

In **Book Two** you will
- Learn several new strumming techniques
- Enlarge your repertoire of chords
- Learn a fingerpicking pattern for songs with
  four beats to a bar
- Develop left-hand techniques

Plenty of exercises and songs are included so you
can put what you learn into practice.

The accompanying **CD** has all of these pieces on it,
with both demonstrations and backing tracks to play
along with. You will learn at a much faster pace if
you listen to the demonstrations before you attempt
these yourself as this will clarify in your mind the
sound for which you're aiming.

Whilst some of the techniques covered in this book
will take only days to learn, others will take longer
to master. If something is not falling into place,
try another technique and revisit it later.

Everyone learns at a different speed but rest assured
that, even if not apparent at first, your practice
will eventually pay off, and by the end of
the book you will know how to add colour
and style to your playing.

Now, let's get started!

Tuning

In this book we will use the most popular ukulele tuning.

G   C   E   A

These are the strings in order:

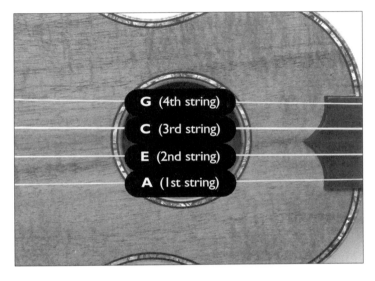

You can refer to the CD to tune each of the strings or use a 'headstock' tuner.

Track 1

Holding your instrument

So far you have probably sat down to play the ukulele as this is the easiest position. However, as you progress through this book try to play whilst standing up. The principles are the same for both positions.

The ukulele should be held gently with the forearm and pressed lightly into the side of your body between your waist and lower ribcage. Apply just enough pressure to keep your ukulele from slipping. The left hand should act as a balance.

Tip

Remember to use a mirror to check your position!

Reminders

Chord boxes

To hold down a chord, apply pressure from your fingertips, pressing into the fingerboard just behind the fret.

Chord boxes are used to illustrate the fingering required for each chord. The heavy dots indicate where to place your fingers. The circle above the diagram indicates that the string is to be played open.

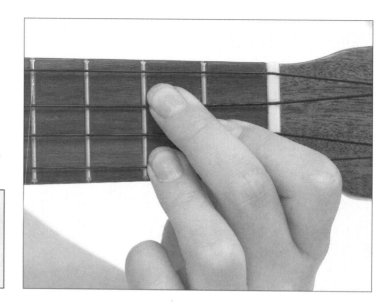

> ## Tip
>
> Whenever you see a window box, imagine turning it on its side to match the way you hold your ukulele.

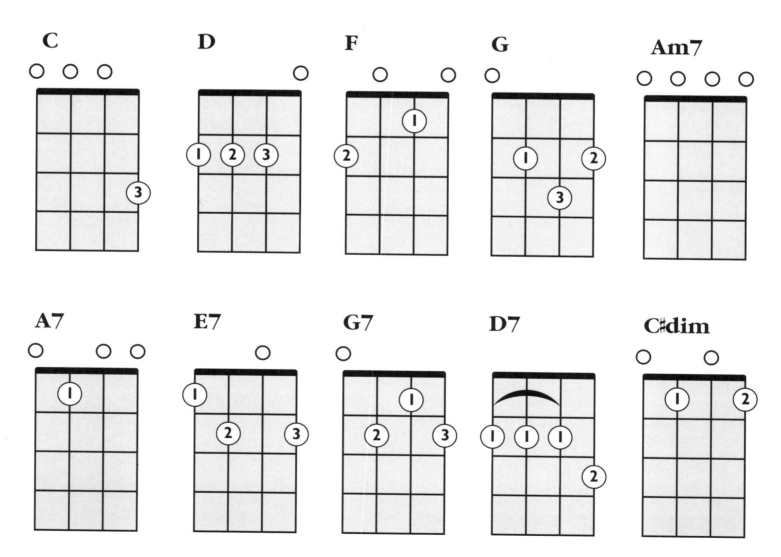

Strumming

A basic strumming style comprises a **downstroke** and an **upstroke**.

Downstroke: Starting from 3–4 inches above the soundhole, strike the strings with the nail of the 1st finger and follow through until 3–4 inches away from the soundhole on the opposite side.

Upstroke: Brush the strings with the soft, fleshy part of the 1st finger, returning to the starting position ready for the next downstroke.

Fingerpicking

In Book One you learnt a simple fingerpicking pattern to use in songs with three beats to a bar.

The pattern consists of six notes, each sounded by plucking an individual string with either the thumb (**T**) or 1st finger (**f1**). One note is played on each beat and half beat in every bar creating a seamless accompaniment to the song.

The diagram below illustrates this pattern.

Having recapped the ground covered in Book One, let's move on to something new!

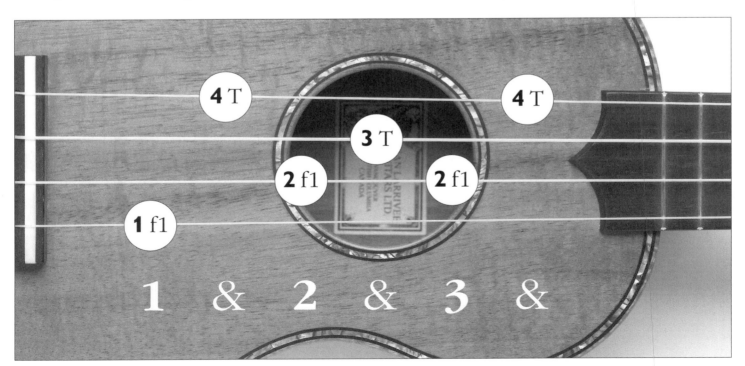

Hawaiian stroke

The Hawaiian stroke (also known as the 'double up strum') is a relaxed sequence of eight strokes and works best with songs that have four beats to a bar. The stroke uses downstrokes and upstrokes, the techniques for which we have already covered. Its unusual characteristic is that it places two upstrokes one after another. This makes it slightly tricky at first, but also gives it a unique sound.

It can be broken down into four beats:

Down

Down, Up

Down, Up, Down

Up, Up

Listen to the demonstration on the CD then try playing this stroke whilst holding down the chord of F.

Track 2

Tip
Give the last upstroke an accent by striking the strings with greater force.

The exercises below give you an opportunity to practise this new strumming pattern. When you are confident, move on and play through the song.

Exercise in F

Track 3

Are you getting the hang of it? It's a cool stroke.

Let's try it again with an Exercise in C.
Watch out for the chord changes midway through the strokes.

Exercise in C

Track 4

 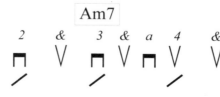 

This happy-sounding strumming pattern is the perfect stroke to use in an introduction or a 'fill' between vocal entries.
You can also use just the second half of the stroke on its own.

If You're Happy And You Know It

Let's see how the stroke works within a song. The strumming pattern in this song alternates between the basic downstroke/upstroke pattern and the new Hawaiian stroke.

Listen to the demonstration track before you play through the song yourself.

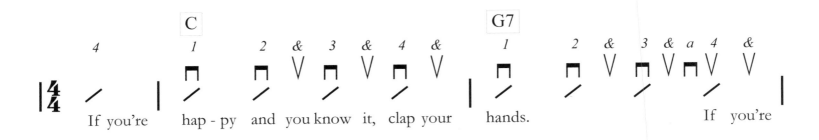

Thumb roll

To learn the thumb roll we need to introduce a new stroking technique.

1

Start with the right hand high above the soundhole and with a large distance between the thumb and 1st finger.

2

Strike the strings with the nail of the 1st finger as you would do for a standard **downstroke**.

3

Follow through with the side of the thumb, hitting the top two or three strings. This creates a 'ripple' sound.

4

Close the gap between the thumb and 1st finger such that the thumb is resting on the finger.

Finish with a standard **upstroke**, brushing the strings with the soft part of the 1st finger in an upward movement, and then a **downstroke**, striking the strings with the nail of the 1st finger. Play these strokes in quick succession.

To commence the stroke again, throw the thumb out as shown in step 1 to create the all-important gap between the thumb and 1st finger.

To summarise, the thumb roll comprises the following four elements:

Downstroke with nail of 1st finger

Follow through with side of thumb

Upstroke with fleshy part of 1st finger

Downstroke with nail of 1st finger

The entire pattern fits into two beats.

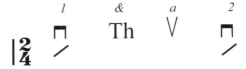

('Th' denotes the follow through with the thumb.)

Listen to the CD to hear the sound you're aiming for. Then try playing this stroke whilst holding down the chord of C.

Track 7

In the following exercise we will couple the thumb roll (two beats) with two downstrokes.

> **Tip**
>
> Remember to 'kick out' the thumb in preparation for each thumb roll.

Exercise in C

Track 8

Generally the thumb roll is used to good effect at a change of chord, usually on the first two beats of a bar.

This lovely stroke can be used in lots of songs and works especially well in driving the rhythm of mid- to up-tempo songs. It is quite tricky to perfect but well worth your perseverance.

London Bridge Is Falling Down

Tracks 9 – 10

Try alternating between downstrokes and the thumb roll in this song.

C

1	2	3	4		1 & a 2	3	4
Lon -	don	Bridge	is		fall - Th ing	down,	

G7

1 & a 2	3	4	**C** 1 & a 2	3	4
fall - Th ing	down,		fall - Th ing	down.	

1	2	3	4		1 & a 2	3	4
Lon -	don	Bridge	is		fall - Th ing	down,	

G7

1 & a 2	3	4	**C** 1	2	3	4
my	fair		la -	dy.		

It's about time we increased the size of our chord bank.

You already know how to play several major chords, but what about minor chords? So far you have only learnt Am7, so let's expand your repertoire.

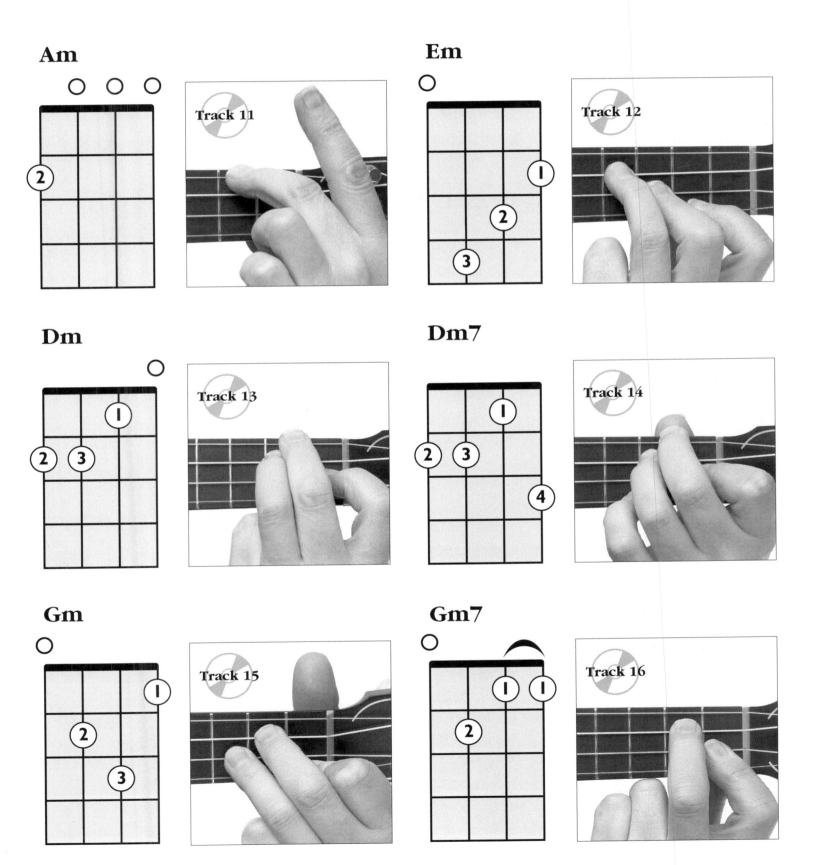

Am
Track 11

Em
Track 12

Dm
Track 13

Dm7
Track 14

Gm
Track 15

Gm7
Track 16

Let's also learn another major chord and some colourful extensions.

B♭

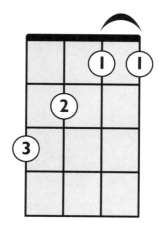 

Track 17

Note that the lowest string is sounding a B♭ when you play this chord. This is the 'root' of the chord and as such we say that this chord is in 'root position'. Remember this when we learn about chord inversions later in the book.

B♭maj7

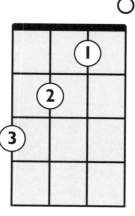 

Track 18

This chord contains the notes of the B♭ major triad (B♭, D and F) and the major 7th (A), unlike B♭7 (also known as the 'dominant 7th') which contains the notes of the major triad (B♭, D and F) and the minor 7th (A♭).

Cmaj7

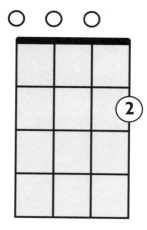 

Track 19

This is another major 7th chord, and as such contains the notes of the C major triad (C, E and G) and the major 7th (B). Try playing this chord in the following sequence to hear the subtle difference between the chords: C—C7—Cmaj7—F.

G6

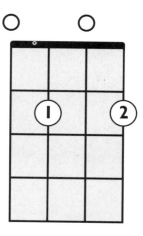 

Track 20

On the following page is an exercise in which you can use some of these new chords.

B♭maj7

| 1 | & | 2 | & | 3 | & | 4 | & |

B♭

| 1 | & | 2 | & | 3 | & | 4 | & |

B♭maj7

| 1 | & | 2 | & | 3 | & | 4 | & |

B♭

| 1 | & | 2 | & | 3 | & | 4 | & |

Am

| 1 | & | 2 | & | 3 | & | 4 | & |

G6

| 1 | & | 2 | & | 3 | & | 4 | & |

Am

| 1 | & | 2 | & | 3 | & | 4 | & |

G6

| 1 | & | 2 | & | 3 | & | 4 | & |

Tip

Listen to the way in which the upstrokes are accented on the CD.

Fingerpicking

Here is a new fingerpicking pattern containing eight notes – one for each beat and half beat in every bar. It therefore fits perfectly with songs that have four beats to a bar.

The pattern looks like this, where each of the beats or half beats corresponds to one of the white circles:

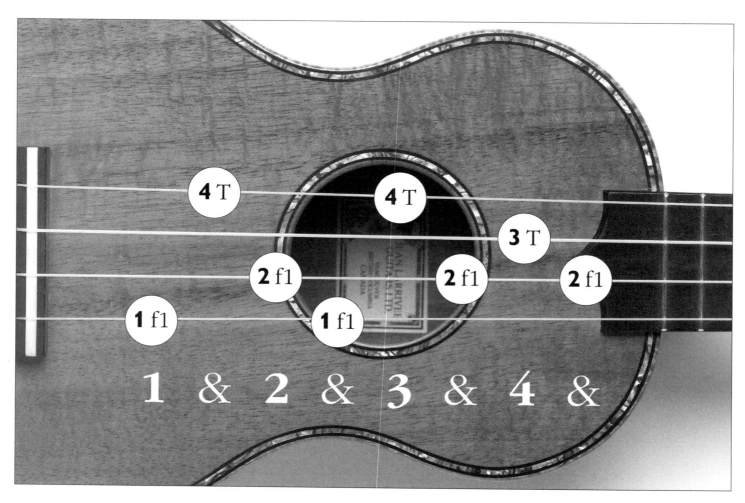

Try the pattern on the chord of C, as shown below:

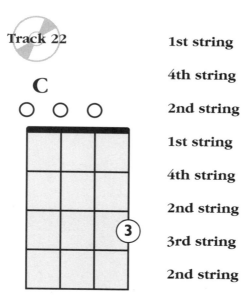

Track 22

C

1st string

4th string

2nd string

1st string

4th string

2nd string

3rd string

2nd string

Remember to use the 1st finger to pluck the 1st and 2nd strings, and the thumb to pluck the 3rd and 4th strings. This includes two consecutive notes that should be plucked with the 1st finger. Can you spot them?

It may sound odd at first but it will start to make sense when you pick up speed!

Tip

You need to use the 1st finger for both the last and first notes of the pattern. This is a little tricky so practise looping it before you try the song on the next page.

On Reflection

C
$\frac{4}{4}$ 1 4 2 1 4 2 3 2

Cmaj7
1 4 2 1 4 2 3 2

Am7
1 4 2 1 4 2 3 2

G6
1 4 2 1 4 2 3 2 :‖

Dm7
1 4 2 1 4 2 3 2

G7
1 4 2 1 4 2 3 2

Dm7
1 4 2 1 4 2 3 2

G7
1 4 2 1 4 2 3 2

C
1 4 2 1 4 2 3 2

Cmaj7
1 4 2 1 4 2 3 2

*You can strum a chord of C
in the last bar.*

Am7
1 4 2 1 4 2 3 2

G6
1 4 2 1 4 2 3 2

C
⊓ ‖

Chord inversions

So far you have learnt just one shape for each chord. It is possible, however, to play a chord in a number of different ways, retaining the same notes but altering the fingering to create a different sound.

These alternative shapes are called 'inversions' and are often positioned further up the fretboard.

They are employed particularly effectively when two or more ukulele players play the same chord, one using the standard shape and the other using an inversion. It's worth learning a few inversions, committing them to memory and then switching between the standard and inverted chord shapes within a song.

Here is the standard chord shape for A7 and the inversion. Both are the chord of A7 but you now have two sounds to choose from!

A7

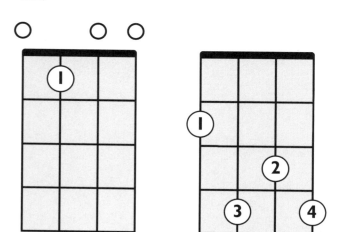

Track 25

Tip

You can use the fleshy part of the thumb to press down on the top string instead of the 1st finger if you prefer. In this set-up place the 2nd finger on the 3rd string, the 1st finger on the 2nd string and the 3rd finger on the bottom string.

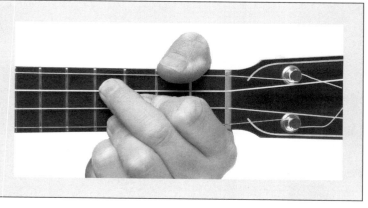

G7

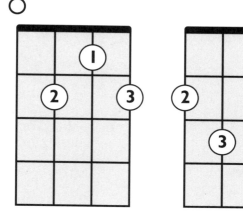

3fr

The number to the right of the chord box indicates that the first finger is to be placed at the 3rd fret. All other fingerings are relative to this.

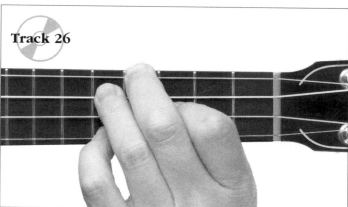

Track 26

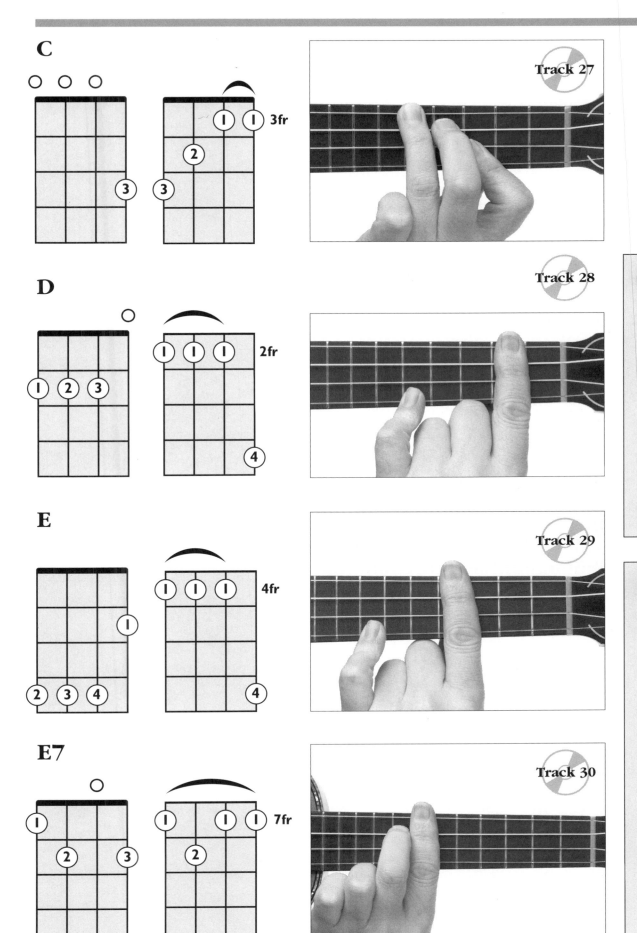

C

Track 27

D

Track 28

E

Track 29

E7

Track 30

Tip

Note that the inverted shape for the chord of E is the same as the inverted shape for the chord of D positioned two frets higher. The shape for the chord of F is the same again, but one fret higher still. Try it!

Tip

The inverted shape for the chord of E7 also uses a 'barre' across all four strings and therefore can be moved up and down the fretboard to sound other chords in the same way as the shape used for the chords of D, E and F. Play around with this shape to see what chords you can find!

Split stroke

This is an amazing strumming technique made famous by George Formby. It is known as the split stroke because it breaks up the rhythm, creating a syncopated feel. The entire pattern is sometimes known as the 'sequence of seven'.

1

Downstroke: Rest the thumb on the 1st finger and keep this finger fairly rigid. This will enable you to hit the strings with force creating accents. Strike all four strings with the nail of the 1st finger.

2

Downstroke: Repeat this accented stroke, again striking all four strings with the nail of the 1st finger.

3

Upstroke: Lightly brush the bottom strings (mainly the 1st string) with fleshy part of the 1st finger. This should sound almost accidental.

4

Downstroke: Strike the top strings (mainly the 4th string) with the nail of the 1st finger. Don't worry if you hit the neighbouring strings when aiming for the top string; the important aspect of the stroke is the timing as this is critical to creating a syncopated feel.

5

Downstroke: Strike all four strings with the nail of the 1st finger. Strike the strings with force to create an accent.

6

Upstroke: Lightly brush the bottom strings (mainly the 1st string) with fleshy part of 1st finger.

7

Downstroke: Strike the top strings (mainly the 4th string) with the nail of the 1st finger.

Tip

Listen to George Formby using this stroke on
'Riding In The TT Races' and 'Our Sergeant Major'.

To summarise, the split stroke comprises the following seven steps:

Downstroke hitting all four strings (accented)

Downstroke hitting all four strings (accented)

Upstroke brushing mainly 1st string

Downstroke hitting mainly 4th string

Downstroke hitting all four strings (accented)

Upstroke brushing mainly 1st string

Downstroke hitting mainly 4th string

Deliver this stroke with attitude; you're the boss of your ukulele!

The entire strumming pattern fits into four beats, the first downstroke lasting a whole beat and then followed by a stroke on each beat and half beat.

Listen to the CD to hear the sound you're aiming for. There are slow and up-to-speed versions. Then try playing this stroke whilst holding down the chord of C.

Tracks 31 – 32

Tip

It's vital that the movement required for this stroke comes from your wrist rather that your arm in order to retain control and speed, and to avoid your arm aching! Keep your wrist loose and relaxed, and check your action in a mirror.

Like many other strumming patterns the split stroke can be adapted, either by shortening or lengthening a section, in order to fit the piece of music you are playing. The last four strokes, which fit into two beats, work especially well on their own. The stroke can be used in up-tempo numbers and slow songs alike, not just Formby tracks.

In the following exercise we will change chord between each stroke.

Exercise in F

Track 33

What Shall We Do With The Drunken Sailor?

George Formby 'borrowed' the tune of this famous sea shanty and re-worked it into a new song, 'On The HMS Cowheel'. Listen to this track if you can.

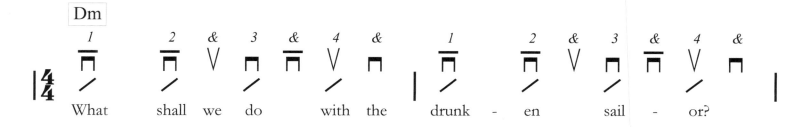

Dm

What shall we do with the drunk - en sail - or?

C

What shall we do with the drunk - en sail - or?

Dm

What shall we do with the drunk - en sail - or,

A7   **Dm**

ear - ly in the morn - ing?

Fan stroke

The fan stroke is another technique popularised by George Formby. It's similar to the split stroke and is equally visually impressive.

1

Downstroke: Strike all four strings with the nail of the 1st finger. (Refer to the instruction and photo on p7 if you need further guidance.)

2

a) Return the right hand to a starting position 3–4 inches above the soundhole and rotate the wrist clockwise, spreading out the fingers like a fan.

b) Flick the top strings with the little finger and ring finger.

3

a) Follow through with the fleshy part of the thumb.

b) Close up the fingers into the palm of the hand.

4

Upstroke: Strike all four strings with the thumbnail.

5

Spread out the fingers and flick the top strings again. (See Step 2.)

6

Again, following through with the fleshy part of the thumb. (See Step 3.)

To summarise, the fan stroke comprises the following:

Downstroke with nail of 1st finger

Fan fingers and **flick** top strings

Follow through with thumb

Upstroke with thumbnail

Fan fingers and **flick** top strings

Follow through with thumb

The whole sequence fits into four beats.

('Fl' denotes the action of flicking the top strings preceded by the fan.)

Listen to the slow and fast demonstrations on the CD and then try this stroke on the chord of C.

Tracks 36 – 37

Exercise in F

Track 38

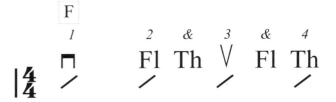

Let's see if we can fit this stroke into 'Oh, Susannah!'.

Other than the fan stroke, this song uses downstrokes. Employ a simple downstroke/upstroke pattern if you prefer.

Oh, Susannah!

C

1	2	3	4	1	2	3	4

4/4 Oh, I come from Al - a - bam - a with my

1	2	3	4	**G7** 1	2 &	3 &	4

ban - jo on my knee.   Fl Th V Fl Th   I'm

C

1	2	3	4	1	2	3	4

go - ing to Lou - si - an - a my

G7

1	2	3	4	**C** 1	2	3	4

true love for to see.   It

1	2	3	4	1	2	3	4

rained all night the day I left, the

G7

1	2	3	4	1	2 &	3 &	4

weath - er it was dry.   Fl Th V Fl Th   The

C | 1 2 3 4 | 1 2 3 4

sun   so   hot,   I | froze   to   death,   Su -

G7 | 1 2 3 4   **C** | 1 2 3 4

- san - nah   don't   you | cry.

F | 1   2 & 3 & 4   (Fl Th V Fl Th) | 1 2 3 4

Oh,   Su - | san - nah,   oh

C | 1 2 3 4   **G7** | 1   2 & 3 & 4   (Fl Th V Fl Th)

don't   you   cry   for | me,   for   I

C | 1 2 3 4 | 1 2 3 4

come   from   Al - a - | bam - a   with   my

G7 | 1 2 3 4   **C** | 1 & 2 & 3 & 4   (V Fl Th V Fl Th)

ban - jo   on   my | knee.

Flamenco stroke

This fun stroke has a Spanish guitar look and sound to it. It's related to the fan stroke but relies on all four fingers as well as the thumb to create a harsh sound and hence a dramatic strumming pattern. Unlike the fan stroke, it works best in songs with three beats to a bar.

1

Downstroke: Strike all four strings with the nail of the 1st finger.

2

a) Return the right hand to a starting position 3–4 inches above the soundhole and separate the fingers, angling the fingertips towards the body of the ukulele.

b) Sweep the strings downwards with the fingers.

3

a) Follow through with the fleshy part of the thumb.

b) Close up the fingers into the palm of the hand.

4

Upstroke: Strike all four strings with the soft part of the 1st finger.

5

Downstroke: Strike all four strings with the nail of the 1st finger.

Tip

This stroke will sound much better if you have good nails!

To summarise, the flamenco stroke comprises the following:

Downstroke with nail of 1st finger

Fan fingers and **sweep** the strings

Follow through with thumb

Upstroke with fleshy part of 1st finger

Downstroke with nail of 1st finger

The whole sequence fits into three beats.

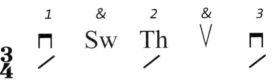

('Sw' denotes the action of sweeping the strings preceded by the fan.)

Listen to the slow and fast demonstrations on the CD and then try this stroke on the Spanish-sounding chord of B♭maj7.

Tracks 41 – 42

Exercise in F

Track 43

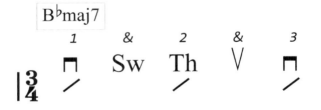

Scarborough Fair

This song has a waltz-like feel with three beats to each bar. This suits the flamenco stroke very well.

To keep things simple this song uses just downstrokes between the flamenco strokes.

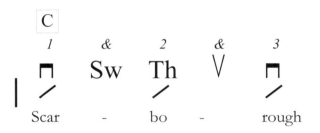

Dm

1	*&*	*2*	*&*	*3*		*1*	*2*	*3*
⊓	Sw	Th	V	⊓		⊓	⊓	⊓
/		/		/		/	/	/
Are				you		go -	ing	to

C

1	*&*	*2*	*&*	*3*		**Dm**		
						1	*2*	*3*
⊓	Sw	Th	V	⊓		⊓	⊓	⊓
/		/		/		/	/	/
Scar -	bo -			rough		Fair?		

1	*&*	*2*	*&*	*3*		**F**		
						1	*2*	*3*
⊓	Sw	Th	V	⊓		⊓	⊓	⊓
/		/		/		/	/	/
Pars -				ley,		sage,		rose -

G7

1	*&*	*2*	*&*	*3*		**Dm**		
						1	*2*	*3*
⊓	Sw	Th	V	⊓		⊓	⊓	⊓
/		/		/		/	/	/
- mar -	y			and		thyme.		Re -

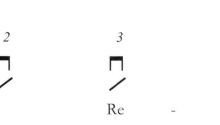

F

1	*&*	*2*	*&*	*3*		*1*	*2*	*3*
⊓	Sw	Th	V	⊓		⊓	⊓	⊓
- mem		-		ber		me		to

Dm   C

1	*&*	*2*	*&*	*3*		*1*	*2*	*3*
⊓	Sw	Th	V	⊓		⊓	⊓	⊓
one		who		lives		there;		

Dm   C

1	*&*	*2*	*&*	*3*		*1*	*2*	*3*
⊓	Sw	Th	V	⊓		⊓	⊓	⊓
she				was		once		a

Dm

1	*&*	*2*	*&*	*3*		*1*	*2*	*3*
⊓	Sw	Th	V	⊓		⊓	⊓	⊓
true		love		of		mine.		

Left-hand techniques

Slides

It is possible to move between two chords which share the same chord shape but are positioned at different points on the fretboard by sliding between them. This creates a unique sound.

Listen to the CD and then follow the instructions below to slide between the chords of G♭ and G.

Track 46

1

G♭

With the fingers in the position for the chord of G♭ strike the strings.

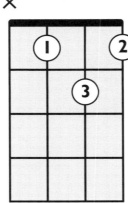

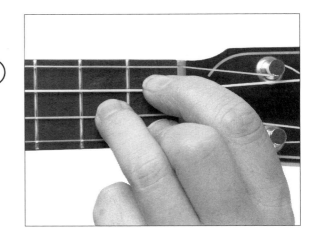

2

Retaining the chord shape, slide the fingers up the fretboard to the position for the chord of G.

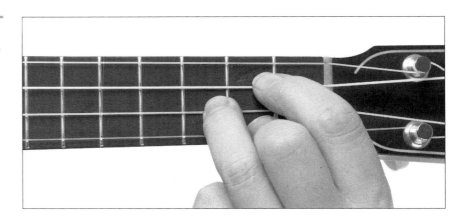

3

G

Don't strike the strings again, instead let the 'echo' ring the chord as the left hand moves up the fretboard.

Now try sliding between the inverted positions for the chords of D♭7 and D7. Refer to the chord dictionary for the relevant shapes.

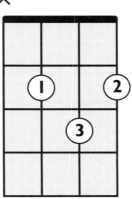

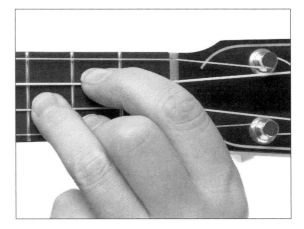

Damping

Also known as 'vamping', this term describes the technique of releasing and re-applying pressure on the strings quickly and repeatedly.

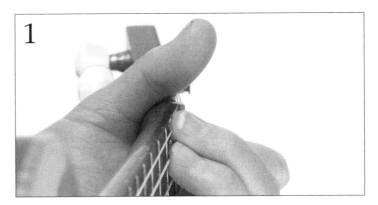

1

With the fingers in the position for the chord of Dm7 strike the strings.

2

Gently release the pressure on the strings from the fingertips almost, but not quite, 'letting go' of the shape.

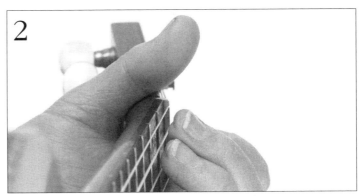

3

Re-apply the pressure on the strings from the fingertips very quickly.

Repeat this sequence of releasing and re-applying the pressure several times in quick succession.

Listen to the effect this creates.

 Track 47

Let's use these techniques in an exercise. Slide between the chords of G♭ and G, and between the chords of D♭7 and D7. Employ the damping effect on the 2nd and 3rd beats of each bar.

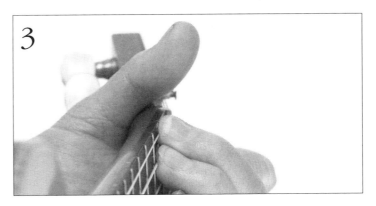

Exercise in F

 Track 48

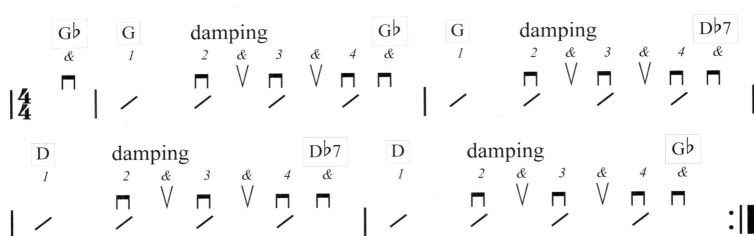

Bobby Shaftoe

This song uses a number of the strokes we have
looked at in this book. You could also try using some
of the new inverted chord shapes you have learnt,
perhaps for the chord of C7.

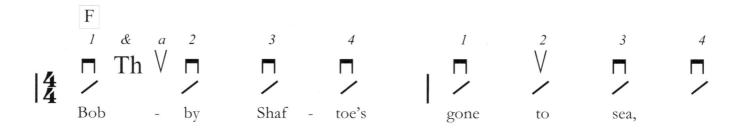

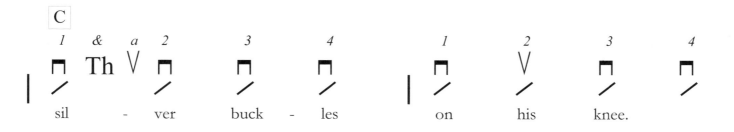

F

1	2	&	3	&	4	&	1	2	3	4

Bob   -   by   Shaf   -   toe's   bright   and   fair,

C7

1	2	&	3	&	4	&	1	2	3	4

comb   -   ing   down   his   yel   -   low   hair.

F

1	2	3	4	1	&	a	2	3	4

He's   my   own   for   ev   -   er   -   more,

Th

C7

1	2	&	3	&	4	1	2	3	4

bon   -   ny   Bob   -   by   Shaf   -   toe.

Fl   Th   Fl   Th

F

Happy playing!

The song 'Bobby Shaftoe', on the previous page, serves as a great summary of what we have covered in this book. You may not have perfected each technique yet but keep practising and you'll only get better!

Remember that listening to recordings of great ukulele players such as George Formby will also aid your progress as a player, and that there is much to be gained from sharing your newfound love of the ukulele with others either as part of a club, an ensemble or an online community.

Thank you for buying this book. I hope you feel that you are developing as a ukulele player and that you are still having fun with it.

Enjoy!

Steven Sproat
www.stevensproat.com

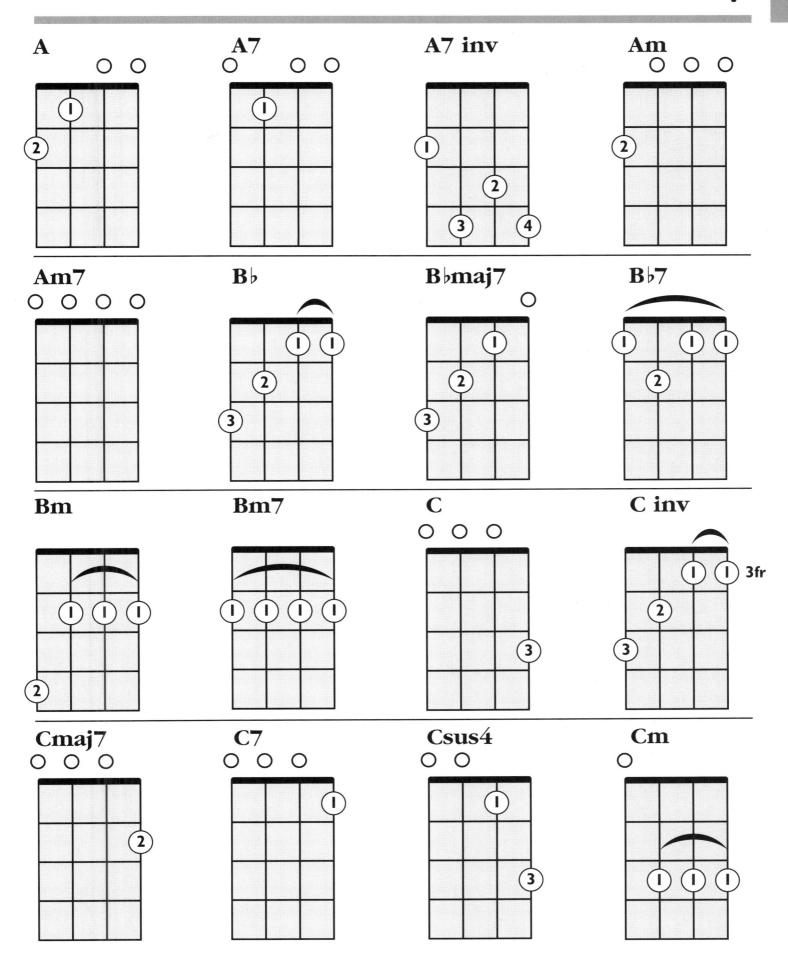

Chord dictionary

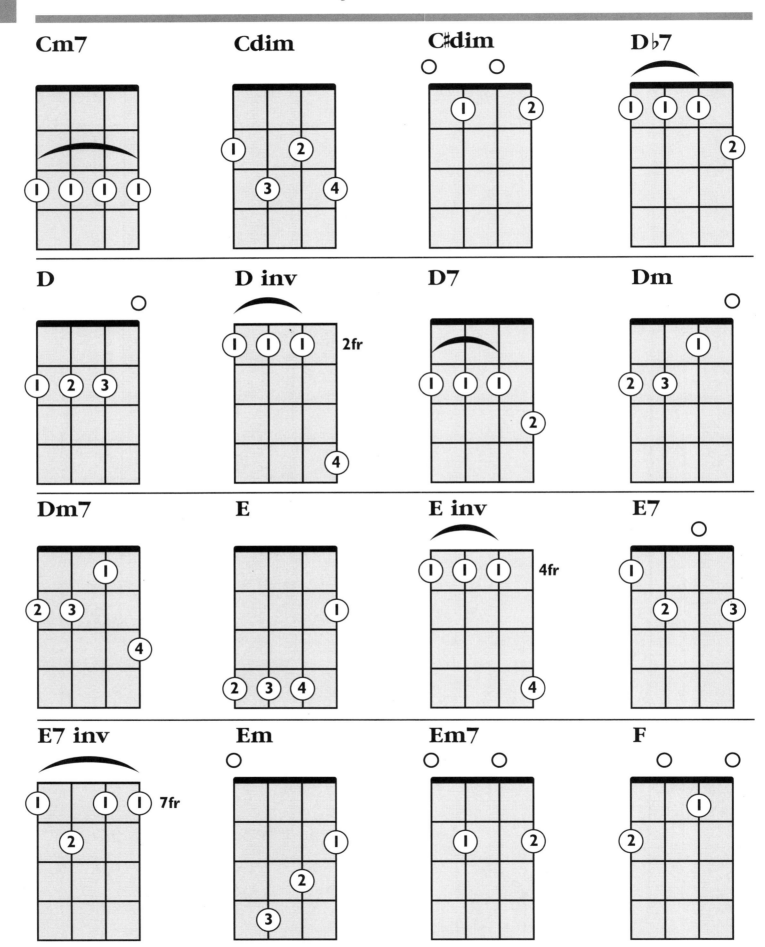

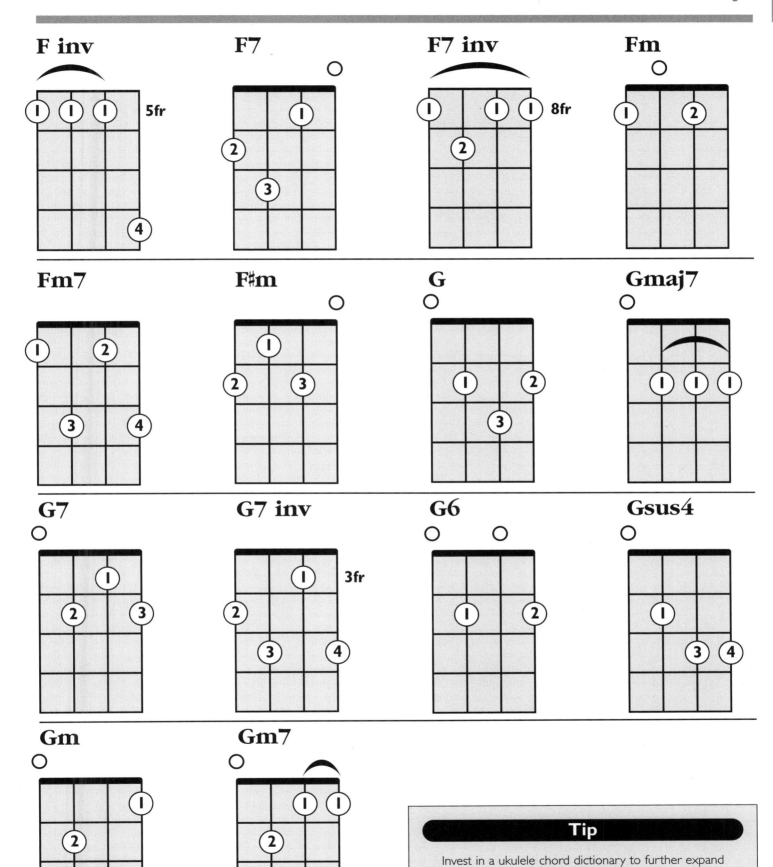

Tip

Invest in a ukulele chord dictionary to further expand your repertoire of chords, enabling yourself to play even more songs.

CD Track Listing

1 Tuning notes

2 Hawaiian stroke (chord of F)

3 Hawaiian stroke: Exercise in F

4 Hawaiian stroke: Exercise in C

5 If You're Happy And You Know It

6 If You're Happy And You Know It *Backing Track*

7 Thumb roll (chord of C)

8 Thumb roll: Exercise in C

9 London Bridge Is Falling Down

10 London Bridge Is Falling Down *Backing Track*

11 Chord of Am

12 Chord of Em

13 Chord of Dm

14 Chord of Dm7

15 Chord of Gm

16 Chord of Gm7

17 Chord of B♭

18 Chord of B♭maj7

19 Chord of Cmaj7

20 Chord of G6

21 New chords: Exercise

22 Fingerpicking (chord of C)

23 On Reflection

24 On Reflection *Backing Track*

25 Chord of A7 and A7 inversion

26 Chord of G7 and G7 inversion

27 Chord of C and C inversion

28 Chord of D and D inversion

29 Chord of E and E inversion

30 Chord of E7 and E7 inversion

31 Split stroke (chord of C): Slow

32 Split stroke (chord of C): Fast

33 Split stroke: Exercise in F

34 What Shall We Do With The Drunken Sailor?

35 What Shall We Do With The Drunken Sailor? *Backing Track*

36 Fan stroke (chord of C): Slow

37 Fan stroke (chord of C): Fast

38 Fan stroke: Exercise in F

39 Oh, Susannah!

40 Oh, Susannah! *Backing Track*

41 Flamenco stroke (chord of B♭maj7): Slow

42 Flamenco stroke (chord of B♭maj7): Fast

43 Flamenco stroke: Exercise in F

44 Scarborough Fair

45 Scarborough Fair *Backing Track*

46 Slides

47 Damping

48 Left-hand Techniques: Exercise

49 Bobby Shaftoe

50 Bobby Shaftoe *Backing Track*